TWO LECTURES

UPON THE

RELATIONS OF CIVIL LAW

TO

CHURCH POLITY, DISCIPLINE, AND PROPERTY.

BY

HON. WILLIAM STRONG, LL.D.

JUSTICE OF THE SUPREME COURT, U. S.

NEW YORK:

DODD & MEAD, PUBLISHERS,

751 BROADWAY.

PREFACE.

THE two following lectures were delivered, by request, before the faculty and students of the Union Theological Seminary in New York, during the winter of 1874–'5. In preparing them, it was not the purpose of the author to make a full, orderly, and elaborate exposition of the subject intended to be presented. Neither the time nor the space he was at liberty to use, was sufficient for such an exposition. But it was his effort to give to those who heard him, such information as he regarded quite important for them to have, respecting the general principles of municipal or civil law bearing upon the polity of churches in this country, and upon their discipline and property. Courts of law in the several States of the Union are not unfrequently occupied by controversies in which these principles are involved, and it is believed to be important that ministers and other officers of churches should have some acquaintance with them. Such knowledge would, in many cases, tend to relieve them from embarrassment, and enable them to avoid the unhappy litigation by which the peace and prosperity of churches is so much disturbed. In the hope that what I have said in these lectures may prove useful to others than those who heard them, they are now given to the press.

W. STRONG.

FIRST LECTURE.

Gentlemen of the Seminary :—

In attempting to exhibit before you some of the organized rules of civil or municipal law, I find myself embarrassed by several considerations. One is found in the fact that abstract legal discussions are proverbially dry and uninteresting to those who have not made the law a subject of considerable investigation. Such persons cannot be expected to discover, at once, how far-reaching a single principle may be, what relation it bears to a system wide enough to embrace all human conduct in social life, and how necessary it is to observe carefully distinctions apparently minute and unimportant, yet really significant and potential in results. There are few minds for which the abstract has any attractions. Even for the student whose purpose it is to adopt the law as a profession, a resolute will is needed to overcome the disrelish he is sure to encounter in the earlier stages of his investigations. It is related of a distinguished English lawyer that, when consulted by a father respecting the qualifications necessary for his son's attaining success at the bar, he replied by the inquiry, "Can your son eat sawdust without butter?" I know, however that the uninteresting nature of my subject ought not to embarrass me. That which Mr. Chitty described as "sawdust without butter" is not unnutritious food. In multitudes of instances it has proved an element of power and of usefulness. It by no means follows that, because a subject to which we devote our attention is difficult and uninteresting, it is therefore unprofitable. It is often true, in our riper years as it was in our boyhood, that the studies which have least attraction for us, are those which we most need to pursue; those which tend in the highest degree to our mental development and to our efficiency in life.

Other sources of the embarrassment which I feel, are found in the difficulty of selecting the particular topics to which your attention may most profitably be directed, and in the impossibility of thoroughly discussing any subject, selected within the assigned limits of these lectures. Selection is indispensable. Municipal law is a very large and comprehensive subject. It embraces all the numerous relations which men sustain to each other in a state of civil society. It cannot well be understood without knowledge of its history and development. Moreover, it is a system no part of which can be thoroughly comprehended without acquaintance with every other part, and without some conception of it as a whole. It has sometimes been said to be the accumulated common sense of the wisest men of many generations applied to the affairs of social life, and adapted to that life's innumerable relations. Like everything human, it is also undergoing constant changes to meet the ever-changing conditions and wants of civil society. Among its maxims are some, doubtless, which do not commend themselves to the entire approbation of the age in which we live. Yet even these are accepted rules of civil conduct, and they are not without support in sound reason. They are as controlling as if they commanded universal approval. For every civil relation, municipal law prescribes a system of rules together constituting what is believed to be the most just and convenient regulation of human conduct therein. To enumerate these rules, or to trace the modifications they have undergone, would be impossible within the limits of the most extended course of lectures. It would be the labor of a lifetime. Yet something may be accomplished in a very brief period. Though to make ourselves thoroughly acquainted with the science of civil law; with its general principles, or framework, and with the details of its structure, requires (to use the words of a distinguished English judge), more than the "lucubrationes viginti annorum," we can, by making use of fragments of time, partially explore one of its departments, and make discoveries that will not be without their use. This is all I propose to attempt in these lectures.

There are some of the rules of civil law with which, in my judgment, those who intend entering the Christian ministry ought to be acquainted. Ignorance of them has, I know, in some cases, proved embarrassing, and has led to unhappy mistakes. I am aware it has sometimes been said: Partial knowledge tends to error; and to a limited extent this may be true. Another maxim often quoted is "A little knowledge is a dangerous thing, drink deep, or taste not, etc." From this I entirely dissent. Undervaluing not in the least the worth of thorough acquaintance with every subject in regard to which knowledge is sought,

I still maintain that even imperfect knowledge is better than none. All our knowledge is imperfect. There is no subject in morals or in law, the extremest depths of which man has ever sounded. The unknown greatly transcends the known. But even partial knowledge is power, if, so far as it extends, it be accurate. In the hope, therefore, that what I may say will prove useful, though it be not a full exposition of all that may be known of the subject, I invite your attention to some remarks upon a branch of civil law, some knowledge of which, I assume, you may desire to possess. It is the relation which civil, or municipal law sustains, in this country, to church polity, discipline, and property. That some such relation does exist, may be inferred from what I have already said, but precisely what it is, and to what particulars it extends, is not easily defined. Certainly it is far less intimate in this country than it is in any other country where the common, or the civil law, is recognized.

Great Britain, from which we have derived the great body of our laws, has a legally established form of church organization connected with the government; as well as a form of doctrine; a religion of state. The polity of the church, as well as its discipline and property, are subordinate to the government and are regulated by it. And in the continental countries of Europe, the church is also supported by laws, and has a close connection with the state. In England, the polity of the established church rests in large measure upon the civil law, and no substantial change or modification of it can be made without the consent of the government. Its bishops are appointed by the crown, and they have a seat in Parliament as bishops, or lords spiritual. The church is dependent for its support upon the civil law, its discipline is controlled or supervised by the state, and its property is held and governed by the rules of the common law. Dissent is tolerated, it is true, but the relation of the civil government to the established church is almost as intimate as is that of one of our State governments to a corporation created by it.

In the United States there is no union of church and state, and, there never can be any without a change in our organic laws. The amendments of the Federal Constitution adopted in 1789 expressly ordain that "no religious test shall ever be required as a qualification for any civil office or public trust under the United States, and that Congress shall make no law respecting an establishment of religion, or prohibiting the free exercise thereof." These, it is true, are restrictions only upon the power of the general government. They are not operative upon the several States. But in almost all, if not in all, the constitutions of the several States may be found ordinances of similar purport. I presume there is no exception. They are variant in form and in modes of expression, but their purpose and meaning is substantially the same. They declare generally that no preference shall ever be given to one form of church polity over another; or to one denomination over another; that no religious test shall be required as a qualification for office, or for any position of trust, and that involuntary payments for the support of any religious teacher, or for the erection of any religious edifice, shall not be compelled. They declare it to be the right of all men to worship God in any manner, at all times, according to the dictates of their own conscience. The words of the constitution of Delaware well express the general sense of all the provisions relative to this subject which have been incorporated into the fundamental laws of the different States, though they are less explicit than some others. After premising that men have a natural right to worship and to serve their Creator according to the dictates of their consciences; that it is the duty of all men frequently to assemble together for the public worship of the Author of the universe, and that purity and morality, on which the prosperity of communities depends, are thereby promoted, that constitution declares that "no man shall or ought to be compelled to attend any religious worship; or to the maintenance of any ministry against his own free will and consent, and that no power shall, or ought to be vested in, or assumed by, any magistrate that shall in any case interfere with, or in any manner control, the rights of conscience in the free exercise of religious worship, nor shall any preference be given by law to any religious societies, denominations, or modes of worship."

By the third section of the ninth article of the constitution of Pennsylvania, it is ordained, "that all men have a natural and indefeasible right to worship Almighty God according to the dictates of their own consciences; that no man can of right be compelled to attend, erect, or support any place of worship, or to maintain any ministry against his consent; no human authority can in any case whatever control, or interfere with, the rights of conscience; and no preference shall ever be given by law to any religious establishment or modes of worship." I refer to no others. These are fair samples of what may be found in the fundamental law of the States generally. They are acknowledgments of natural and indefeasible rights, and they are disclaimers of governmental powers claimed and exercised in Great Britain, as well as on the continent of Europe.

These provisions in the Federal and State constitutions, it is obvious, have rendered impossible any such close relation between civil government and church polity and discipline as now exists in England, and elsewhere, and they greatly restrict, if they do not forbid, interference by the law, not merely with individual faith, but with the external and internal affairs of church organization, including church discipline.

This renunciation of civil authority over ecclesiastical organizations is the assertion of a doctrine not always accepted even in this country. It was not accepted by most of the colonies in their early existence, by most of them even at the time of the American revolution. Down to that period there was a much closer connection between the church and the state than now exists. The church in the colonies was largely supported by the civil law, and its organization, as well as the right to membership in it, was often the subject of provincial legislation, and received the attention of the magistracy.

Indeed, it is only within the last forty years that a complete divorce has been effected in some of the States, and that the principles asserted in the Federal Constitution, as well as in those of the States, have been accepted in their full meaning.

The history of this change in the relation of the civil law to church polity and discipline would be interesting and instructive, had I time to follow it through all its course. I can but briefly notice it. It was quite in accordance with what might have been expected that the earlier settlers of the country, who came principally from England, brought with them the law under which they had been trained. And that they did bring with them the compulsory usages of their fatherland, that common law which regulated civil conduct generally, is well known.

They knew no other. They had been accustomed to the existence of a church closely connected with the state, and subordinate, in many particulars, to the king, to parliament, and to the civil magistracy. It was very natural that they should adopt a similar system, with such modifications only as their altered circumstances, their religious faith, and their experience, suggested. Accordingly, almost at the first, some of the colonial legislatures began to enact laws respecting the church, in imitation of the laws of England. Their enactments extended to church organization, to the erection of parishes with defined boundaries, to provision for the support of a ministry, to furnishing places for public worship, to compelling attendance upon such worship and even to the denunciation of penalties against false doctrine and heresy. In Massachusetts, parishes were created only by order of the General Court. Their metes and bounds were defined by law. They were ecclesiastical precincts, as fully as English parishes are, though in many cases corresponding with township divisions. It was recognized as an obligation proper to be imposed by the civil law that every man inhabiting a parish or town, or having lands therein, should pay taxes for the support of the Gospel within that town or precinct, and such taxes were imposed by statutes. Each town or parish was required by law to have a minister, a meeting-house, and a parsonage, and, in case of neglect to furnish them and to provide for the maintenance of the minister, the county court was empowered to order what maintenance should be allowed, and to issue warrants to assess taxes upon the inhabitants, which the constables were required to collect like any other town taxes. From such orders of the county courts appeals to the General Court were also authorized. Penalties were imposed upon towns for neglect to supply "able and faithful preaching" to the people. Fines were levied by law for absence from public worship, and judges of county courts were enjoined by statute to attend to the orders of the General Court concerning purging the towns from such ministry and public teachers as should be found vicious in their lives and perniciously heterodox in their doctrine. Magistrates were also authorized to impose punishments upon those who, in their opinion, were guilty of error or heresy, and the right of persons to vote in all parish, or ecclesiastical matters, was regulated by the civil law. All this exhibits a very close connection between the church and the state, almost complete subordination of the church to the state in matters of polity, of discipline, of support, and even of faith.

In most of the other colonies a very similarly close relation existed between the civil law and the church. This is especially true of those in New England, excepting Rhode Island. Nor was such legislation confined to the provinces mainly settled by the Puritans. There were differences in detail, but the right of the state to direct church organization, discipline and support, as well as to control doctrine, to some extent, appears nowhere (except perhaps in Rhode Island) to have been seriously questioned. By the charter of liberties of New York, established by the General Assembly in 1683, under the Duke of York, complete enjoyment of religious doctrine and worship was accorded only to persons who professed their faith in God by Jesus Christ. I am not aware that the political rights of freemen were denied to those who were not members of some orthodox church in the province, as they were in some other colonies. But in many other respects the early legislation of New York relating to ecclesiastical matters was much like that of Massachusetts. In some particulars it was more remarkable. For very many years the civil governor was authorized to collate any person to any church, chapel, or other ecclesiastical benefice within the province, as often as any of them happened to be void, and all religious ministers were required to be commissioned by the government. Even down to the time of the revolution, Dutch and Presbyterian churches found great difficulty in obtaining grants of charters.

The first code of laws of Virginia enjoined that religion be established in the province according to the doctrine and rites of the church of England, and thus the English Episcopal church became the church of the State. Strict conformity was required by the statute law, and every inhabitant was compelled to contribute for the support of the established church. Civil law directed vestry men to be chosen in every parish; the whole liturgy to be read thoroughly in public worship, and denounced banishment as the penalty of teaching, even in private, by non-conformists. No marriage ceremony was tolerated, except performed according to the rubric in the book of common prayer. Fines were imposed upon Quakers for meeting in conventicles of their own, and for absence from the service of the established church, and schismatics were subjected to penalties for refusing to have their children baptized. These harsh provisions of the law, it is true, were not all of long continuance, but there was in Virginia, down to the period of the revolution, a close alliance between the civil government and the church.

In East Jersey religious liberty was confined to Protestant professors of the Christian faith, and the legislature of West Jersey prescribed a confession of faith as a condition of holding office. Indeed I feel justified in asserting, after considerable examination of the colonial laws, that nearly all the colonies, at some period of their history, undertook to regulate ecclesiatical affairs as fully as if their power over those affairs had been absolute and unlimited.

I have not time to pursue this reference to historical facts further. Enough has been said to show that, with rare exceptions, the colonies all claimed and exercised the right to control religious faith, church order, and discipline, and asserted complete supremacy over church organizations. It was not until they were brought into intimate political union with each other in the revolutionary struggle; not until they were threatened with common dangers from abroad; when it became apparent that their safety depended upon their perfect harmony of feeling and action, and not until they were led to see how difficult, if not impossible, it would be for them to unite on any common platform of religious faith or church order, being as they were, Congregationalists or Independents in New England, Presbyterians and Friends in Pennsylvania and New Jersey, Roman Catholics in Maryland, and Episcopalians in the South—not until then, that they accepted the modern doctrine which recognizes perfect religious liberty and equality before the law, without the existence of any power in the state to regulate or control church establishment or church discipline. Before that time indeed, the church had been completely divorced from the state in some of the colonies, but then its independence became generally an accepted doctrine. It found a place at once in several of the constitutions which superseded the colonial charters; and in the celebrated ordinance of 1787, for the government of the territory of the United States north and west of the Ohio, it was declared to be an article of compact between the original States and the people and States in the territory—a fundamental principle to remain forever unalterable, that no person demeaning himself in a peaceable manner should ever be molested on account of his mode of worship, or religious sentiments. This was before the adoption of the Federal Constitution, and it was soon followed by the declarations I have quoted from that instrument, and by the more explicit declaration in the organic laws of the several States.

But, notwithstanding this complete renunciation of authority in the state to prescribe any form of church government, or to control, or interfere with the internal management of any church organization, or to make provision for its support, or for the support of its ministers; notwithstanding perfect religious freedom is now, in this country, everywhere secured by bills of rights incorporated into the fundamental laws of the land, it is not to be inferred that the civil law has no longer any relation to the church—to either its polity, its discipline, or its property. On the contrary, it is still true that the law recognizes the existence of the church as an important element of civil society. It acknowledges and protects its right to exist, and to enjoy the possession of privileges and powers. It recognizes also the discipline of the church, by which I mean, not merely its correction and punishment of its members, but also its maintenance of church order and internal regulation. It does not undertake to determine whether one religious association is more truly the church than another, or to allow to one a preference over another, but it permits each to make its own rules and to enforce them. It protects every church in the enjoyment of rights of property, and whenever those rights are invaded it furnishes a remedy. Recognizing the indefeasible right of any body of men to associate for the worship of God, in accordance with the forms and modes selected by them, it will not allow their assemblies to be disturbed. In many of the States, I think in all, statutes have been enacted against such disturbances, and even where no such statutes exist, it would be regarded as a misdemeanor at law to disturb a religious congregation, a misdemeanor punishable by fine and imprisonment. And, perhaps, it is regarded as an offence of greater enormity to disturb a religious assembly than it would be to create disorder in any other gathering, for the reason that the right to assemble for religious purposes is guaranteed by organic laws. There are few, if any statutes, prohibiting disturbances of other assemblages.

No state recognition of the church, however, or even of religious obligation, is to be inferred from the fact that the civil law punishes many offences which are condemned by the Divine law, and which the church also condemns and punishes. Many offences against civil society are acts prohibited by the Decalogue, and by all churches. False swearing, theft, adultery, and murder, are violations of municipal law, and persons guilty of them are punished by authority of the state, not because the offences are violations of Divine law, or the law of the church, but because they are infractions of the rules which civil society has found it necessary to establish for its own protection. In many of the States, orderly observance of the Sabbath, and abstinence from unnecessary labor, are enjoined by statutes. Penalties are also denounced against profaneness and blasphemy. But it would be a mistake to regard such enactments as church recognitions. They may have been suggested by respect for religion, but as civil enactments they are justifiable only by their tendency to protect the public peace, and to preserve public decency, good order, and good morals—objects for which civil society exists. Whether it be true, as has been held by some courts (notably the highest courts of New York and Pennsylvania), and as has been declared by very many eminent judges, that Christianity is, in a limited sense, a part of the common law of the land, or whether it be not true, "it is still consistent with every guaranty of the rights of conscience and religious liberty to hold that it is the popular religion of the country, an insult to which tends to the disturbance of the public peace. The laws and institutions of all the States are built on the foundation of reverence for Christianity. To this extent at least, it must certainly be considered as settled, that the religion revealed in the Bible is not to be openly reviled or blasphemed, to the annoyance of sincere believers, without responsibility to the civil law."

Apart from this, however, there is abundant evidence that the law in this country recognizes and tolerates the existence of church organizations. I may add that this is true; without any regard to their form, or the details of their structure, or the avowed principles which lie at their foundation. No matter what may be their constitution, or the religious creed adopted, even though it be offensive to the moral sense of the community, the law does not forbid association of those who accept it, nor will it interfere to break up such associations. This statement, however, should be cautiously received, for while it is true as made, it is equally true that the outworking of a vicious creed may be prevented and punished. *That* toleration and that liberty of conscience which the Federal Constitution and the constitutions of the several States have endeavored to secure are not construed so as to excuse acts of licentiousness, or to justify practices inconsistent with the peace or safety of the State. In many of the fundamental laws, this reservation is expressly made. In all, it is implied, if not expressed. No church organization therefore, or church creed, can be made a cover for any act which, by the law of the State, is an offence against the public peace, against good order, and good morals. Civil law controls external conduct, though not articles of faith. For example, I know of no power in the civil government which can prevent the formation of a church (if such an association can be called a church), one of the articles of the creed of which should be that marriage imposes no obligations, and that free intercourse of the sexes is praiseworthy; or (another article), that one in needy circumstances may, without sin, take the property of another to relieve his distresses, against that other's consent. No law exists in this country against such an association. But whenever such principles are acted out, whenever an individual does any act accordant with such a creed, he becomes amenable to the civil law, and neither his church nor his creed can protect him against legal penalties.

The Mormon church furnishes a good illustration of what I mean. It is well known one of the doctrines of that organization, is that polygamy is in harmony with the law of God and commendable. Revolting as such a doctrine is, and demoralizing in its influence, it has not been thought that either the common law or any statute of the United States can break up the organization, or forbid its members from holding and avowing such a belief, or associating for its propagation. But the practice of it, in other words, its outworking, is within the control of the civil law, and acts of Congress have been passed forbidding and punishing plural marriages. It would be idle for a Mormon indicted for bigamy to plead that his second marriage was recognized as lawful by his church, and sanctioned by his own religious convictions.

Thus far I have called your attention mainly to the fact that the civil law tolerates the existence of church organizations with such a polity as their members may choose to adopt, without inquiry into the articles of their faith. I may now add that the law also leaves the internal management of a church exclusively to their own regulations. Regarding them as voluntary associations, it assumes that their members have consented to be bound by the discipline to which they have subjected themselves. So far as that discipline consists in the correction and punishment of members, in suspension from membership, or in entire exclusion from church privileges, the law not only recognizes it, but to a certain extent justifies church action. Thus even a public declaration made pursuant to the rules of order of a church from which a member has been excommunicated because of his commission of an offence regarded as infamous by the law, is justified, and no action of slander can be maintained for such a publication. The law regards the fact that it was made in the exercise of the discipline of the church as a protection to the person who makes it, and allows the church action to give to the announcement a character different from that which it would otherwise wear. This must be understood, however, with the qualification that the act of discipline and its publication are not malicious.

Again, the law recognizes the right of every church to determine finally who are, and who are not its members. Herein is a marked difference between churches and other organizations. In regard to membership of private corporations generally, such as benevolent, beneficial, or literary societies, as well as those which are pecuniary, rights to membership are subjects of legal cognizance, and there is a remedy provided for irregular amotion. Such corporations may be compelled to restore to membership one who has been expelled without regular trial according to the established forms of the corporate organization, and indeed those forms must be strictly complied with, or a court of law will interfere. It will review the proceeding, and insist upon its perfect regularity. But a church is allowed to determine for itself, construing its own organic rules, whether a member has been cut off; and no civil court will inquire whether the amotion was regularly made, or issue a mandamus to compel a restoration. It accepts the decisions of church courts upon questions of membership as not subject to civil law review. At least such is the general rule.

Such is also the case when the question is, Who are the officers of the church?

Upon that inquiry a civil court will not enter, further than to ascertain what the church itself has decided, or whom it recognizes. Whether a man is a minister, an elder, a bishop, or a deacon, cannot be determined in any court of common or statute law. There are however, some qualifications of this statement, to which I shall hereafter refer.

Almost all, if not all, the questions mooted in the civil courts of this country relating to church polity, discipline, officers, or members, have arisen incidentally in controversies respecting church property. Our churches have various forms of organization, and devise rules for their government and discipline, having a bearing, greater or less, upon their rights to the ownership and the disposition of pecuniary interests. The most prominent forms are the Presbyterian, the Congregationalist, or Independent, and the Episcopal. Each of these is ordinarily an interior organization within a religious society. Church property is generally more or less under the control of these societies, the constituents of which, even though not members of the church, have a voice in its acquisition, management, and disposal. It is held by a variety of tenures, and impressed by a variety of trusts. Over these trusts powers are often vested in officers of the church, officers distinct from those of the religious societies. What the trusts are, and whether the powers over them have been rightly exercised, has frequently been a subject for consideration in civil courts, and it must be confessed the decisions have not been harmonious. But whatever they may have been, I think it may safely be asserted as a general proposition, that whenever questions of discipline, of faith, of church rule, of membership, or of office, have been decided by the church in its own modes of decision, civil law tribunals accept the decisions as final, and apply them as made.

The question may here be raised, Can a civil court inquire, and determine for itself, whether a church judicatory was properly constituted, in accordance with the established order of the church organization, and can it disregard its decisions, if, in its opinion, the judicatory appears not to have been thus constituted. This question is at present a pending one in the country, and opinions differ respecting it. On the one side it is argued that the analogy of the law requires the question to be answered in the affirmative. It is said to be an established rule of the common law that when a matter is submitted to the decision of several arbitrators, all must act together, or their decision will be treated as a nullity, and that this is true though it be stipulated by the parties or directed by a statute that a majority may decide. The presence of all at the trial is indispensable, for the reason that the opinions and arguments of each may affect the judgment of the others. Hence a court may always inquire whether a board of arbitrators has been properly constituted.

There is force in their argument. But on the other hand a church court can hardly be likened to an arbitration. It is a creature of the organic law of the church, not the mere appointee of litigants, chosen to act within the limits imposed by them. It is difficult therefore to see why, if it be recognized as a sufficient judicatory by the highest authority in the church, civil tribunals must not accept it as such. If they must not, great confusion may ensue. Their civil law decisions may come into direct conflict with decisions of ecclesiastical tribunals in matters of which the latter have undoubted cognizance. *Then* it may become necessary for a court of law to determine who are proper officers of the church, and even whether persons excommunicated are not still church members, and entitled to all their rights as such; a power which civil courts have never claimed. I do not, however, wish to be understood as expressing any fixed opinion upon this subject.

When I say, as I have said, that the civil law does not interfere with church organization, or with questions of religious faith, it is proper I should call attention to an apparent, though not a real exception. Cases sometimes arise in civil courts in which it becomes necessary to determine which part of a divided church is entitled to the church property, and where a correct decision can be reached only after an examination of the order of the church, or its ecclesiastical connection, or after an investigation of its articles of faith. These cases most frequently occur when a division has taken place in a church which is a member of a larger organization and subject to ecclesiastical authority outside of itself. To such a church, property is sometimes conveyed by deed or will, for the expressed purpose of maintaining a specified form of organization, or while it remains in a particular ecclesiastical connection, or it may be conveyed to a church, the name of which implies a certain form of church government. A donor, or a grantor, has a right to give to the subject of his gift or grant such a direction as he pleases, or impress upon it any religious use which comports with his wishes. Thus property may be settled for the use of a Protestant Episcopal Church, or for the use of a German Reformed Church, or a Presbyterian Church, or, still more specifically, for the use of an Episcopal Church in connection with the Southern diocese in New York, or for a Presbyterian Church in connection with a particular General Assembly. In such a case when controversies arise within the church respecting the ownership or control of property thus conveyed, and a division takes place, courts of law will inquire which party, or which division, adheres to the form of church government, or acknowledges the church connection designated in the conveyance, and adjudge the right to that party. Thus, if the grant be for the erection or maintenance of a German Reformed Church in connection with the synod of Pennsylvania, and a majority of its members resolve to sever the connection of the church with that synod, courts of law will decree that they have forfeited their right to the property, and will adjudge it to the minority that adheres to the synod. So, if the grant be for the use of a Presbyterian church, and a majority of its members determine to become Congregationalists, or Episcopalians, or Methodists, the civil law will interfere and protect the property for the exclusive use of those who remain Presbyterians. Such a church, or religious society is, in the eye of the law, regarded as the trustee of a charity, holding its property in trust for defined persons, or objects, and civil courts will prevent its diversion to other persons, or other uses. It may then be said generally, that the law will not recognize any right in a church endowed in connection with a larger ecclesiastical organization, and in subordination to it, or endowed with reference to any form of church order, or government, to unite with any other organization, or to become independent, or to abandon its order and adopt another. If it makes such a change, it does it at the penalty of losing the property settled upon it. That property the civil courts will adjudge to those members, however few in number they may be, who continue to act in accordance with the ecclesiastical connection and church order which were accepted when the endowment was made; and which were in contemplation of the donor or grantor. Those who adhere and submit to that established order and connection, are recognized as the church endowed, and the title to the property remains in them. When I speak of a church thus endowed, I mean, where the church order or connection is indicated in the instrument by which the property was acquired. This rule of action, well established in the civil courts by a multitude of decisions, it is evident, necessitates an inquiry into the constitution and discipline of the church, not for the purpose of determining whether they are right or wrong, but to enable the court to discover which of the contending parties adheres to the order and connection, or (which is the same thing), to discover for whose use the settlement was made. The inquiry is after a fact essential to the identification of the grantee, and that fact, whatever it may be, when ascertained, becomes controlling.

The same reason which leads to such an investigation, namely, that civil courts will not permit the diversion of a trust, even when held by a religious society, justifies also, in some cases, an inquiry into the articles of faith or doctrines held by a particular church, or by some of its members. When property is held, charged with a trust for the use of a church receiving and maintaining certain religious doctrines, it occasionally happens that its members depart from the faith, and embrace other and contrary doctrines, while still claiming to hold the property. In such a case, very plainly, if the property *can be* retained by them, it is diverted from the use to which it was first settled, and the intent of the donor or grantor is defeated. Such a perversion the civil law will not allow. It will interpose its strongest arm to arrest it. Here, too, as before, the primary inquiry is, has there been a violation of the trust? And that inquiry can be answered only when it has been ascertained what the doctrines were, to the maintenance and propagation of which the church property was devoted, and whether there has been a departure from those doctrines by those who claim a right to the property.

It was early laid down by a celebrated British chancellor (Lord Eldon), and such is now the accepted law of England, that in internal controversies respecting rights to church property, it is the duty of a court (a civil court), to decide in favor of those, whether a minority or a majority of the congregation, who are adhering to the doctrine professed by the congregation, and the form of worship in practice, and also to the form of church government in operation in the church, with which the congregation was connected, at the time the trust was declared. It may perhaps be doubted whether all this is true in its fullest extent in this country. But it is true that when a settlement of property has been made for the use of a church which holds specified doctrines, those members only have an interest in the property, that hold those doctrines, if it can be gathered from the settlement that the maintenance of those doctrines was intended; and a civil court will do whatever is necessary, in case of a division, to ascertain which party holds them.

Now, as I have already said, church endowments are clothed with an almost boundless variety of trusts, relating not only to church organization, ecclesiastical connection, form of government, or order of worship, but to doctrine and articles of faith. Property may be settled for the use of a Trinitarian church, or of an Universalist church, or of a church holding and teaching the doctrine of total depravity, or of one repudiating the doctrine of election, or of one that accepts the Heidelberg catechism, or of one that believes only Sternhold and Hopkins' version of the Psalms ought to be used in public worship. These are specimens of trusts that may be created. They are all lawful, and civil courts will enforce them as made. Every church, or portion of a church, or religious society, holding property must comply with the conditions expressed or implied in the settlement. Take a single illustration. If a Trinitarian church upon which such a settlement has been made—a settlement manifestly having in view Trinitarian doctrines—departs from its faith, if a majority of its members become Unitarians, they forfeit all right to the property, and civil courts will adjudge the whole to the minority (however small) who remain Trinitarians. Religious faith is thus recognized and acted upon as a sufficient foundation for a legal trust.

There are some cases, however, of more difficulty. They are those in which the trust has not been so accurately defined. Let me state an example. The grant may have no expressed reference to any single doctrine. Suppose it be made to a church adhering to the creed of the German Reformed Church, or, still more loosely, for the erection and support of a German Reformed church, without more. Courts of law hold such a grant as creating a trust. But what trust? I answer, one that is twofold in its nature. First, it is for the use of a church that is German Reformed in its form of government, its order, and its discipline. Secondly, it is for a church that holds the creed or articles of faith accepted by the German Reformed Church generally when the grant was made. Both form and doctrine are essential to the existence of a church. Hence in enforcing such a trust, and protecting it, not only is the form of the beneficiary to be considered, but it is indispensable to inquire what were the doctrines of the church when the trust was stamped upon the property, and what are the accepted doctrines of those who claim to be beneficiaries. If there has been any material departure from the acknowledged standards of faith existing when the trust was founded, those who have thus departed are no longer owners, and they will not be recognized as such by courts of law. They will be compelled to surrender the whole to those who adhere to the standards, and if all have departed the property will revert to the donor.

I am aware it was said by a well-known judge, when delivering the opinions of the highest court in one of the States, this rule is not to be interpreted as meaning that no church or religious organization, to which such a grant has been made, can change any material part of its principles, or practices without forfeiting its property. "This," said he, "would be imposing a law upon all churches that is contrary to the very nature of all intellectual and spiritual life, for it would forbid both growth and decay; not prevent, for that is impossible. The guarantee of freedom to religion," he added, "forbids us to understand the rule in that way." From this I earnestly dissent. It was but the opinion of a single judge; not necessary to the case decided, and it is in conflict with all the well-considered decisions in this country and in England. In commenting upon it, another judge has said, "Civil courts which have the supervision and control of all corporations, and unincorporated religious societies or associations, in matters of property must be guided by plainer principles than those to be found in the nature of intellectual and spiritual life. And the constitutional guaranty of religious freedom has nothing to do with the property. It does not guarantee the privilege of stealing churches, or perverting truths, or defeating the will of a donor. It secures to individuals the right of withdrawing from a church, forming a new society, with such creed and government as they may choose to adopt, raising from their own means another fund; and building another house of worship. But it does not confer upon them the right of taking property consecrated to other uses by those who may be sleeping in their graves." 67 Penn, State, 147.

It may then, I think, be considered as undeniable that in all controversies respecting the right to church property, when the deed or will by which it has been acquired indicates that it was the intention of the grantor or devisor the beneficial use of the property should vest in a church having a specified form of government, or connection, or form of worship; or holding certain doctrines, courts of law will institute all the inquiries necessary to determine who were the real beneficiaries intended, and prevent the diversion of the property to any other uses. And in so doing they will, if necessary, investigate the doctrines held, or the religious belief of the members, not for the purpose of passing upon their soundness, or unsoundness, but to identify the persons for whose use the grant or gift was originally intended.

Of course what I have said has no application to a case where the property is held by a church, or religious society, with no specific trust attached to it, or with no other than that it is for a religious use generally. Such cases sometimes arise in independent churches, governed solely by themselves, either by a majority of their members, or by some authority within them, instituted solely by the members. When in such a church the right to the property is in dispute between two divisions, the majority will control, unless some internal authority has been constituted by general assent to decide. Courts of law will not interfere farther than to give effect to the will of the majority, expressed by themselves or by their agents.

I have thus endeavored, briefly as possible, and quite superficially, I know, to exhibit how far the courts of civil law will enter the domain of the church. To sum up what I have said upon this point, even at the hazard of repetition, I may say that civil courts will not interfere with any church organization, connection, order, discipline, or doctrine, nor will it interfere with the ownership of church property, except to enforce its being held in strict subordination to the uses to which it was devoted when it was acquired.

In saying, as I have said, that the civil law will not undertake to determine who are the officers of the church, I must be understood as having spoken only of strictly church officers. There are officers of religious societies, officers in whom frequently the legal titles to the church property is vested, over whom, and over whose actions courts of law claim and exercise jurisdiction. I speak of trustees of the church property. Many religious societies are incorporated, and such corporations are as much under the control of the civil law, as are any other corporate organizations. They are trustees of the property vested in them. In other cases the property is held by natural persons as trustees for the unincorporated church, or unincorporated religious society. The trustees may have been designated by the founder of the trust, or elected by the members of the church, or of the society out of which the church has been gathered. To determine rights of property, it is often necessary to decide who those trustees are, and consequently to inquire unto the validity of the election of those claiming to have been elected. Such inquiries are conducted precisely as similar ones are, when the title of officers of lay corporations is called in question. It is competent for a civil court to review the election, and not only to decide who received the greatest number of votes, but to pass upon the qualifications of the electors. If none but church members may vote, the court can determine whether those who voted were church members, but the rule for such determination must be that which the church has ordained. They must be considered members whom the church recognizes as such. So even in a case where there is no direct question of property in issue a civil court will eject a person not lawfully elected from an office into which he has intruded.

The General Assembly of the Presbyterian Church has a board of trustees, who are elected by the Assembly. They are a corporate body, having charge of the property of the church, holding it, and managing it for the use of the church. It may become, it has become, in the past, a question whether some of those trustees were duly elected, and empowered to act as such. This is not a question of ecclesiastical law; it is exclusively within the jurisdiction of the civil courts. But it must be observed that neither these nor the trustees of any single church, or religious association are church officers. They have charge of the temporalities only, not at all of the spiritual interests. The acknowledged authority which courts of civil law exercise over them is not therefore in any manner inconsistent with the assertion I have made that such courts will not try or decide who are church officers, but will leave that question to be answered by the church itself, and will accept the answer.

Thus far I have spoken mainly of the church only, and of the relation in which it stands to the civil law. I have noticed the religious society, within which the church is generally a distinct organization, only incidentally, for the purpose of exhibiting how far the civil law will take cognizance of the constitution, order, doctrines, and discipline of the church. I propose now to submit some observations respecting religious societies. They may, with sufficient accuracy, be defined to be voluntary associations of individuals or families united for the purposes of having a common place of worship, providing teachers for instruction in religious doctrines and duties, as well as for the administration of the ordinances of the church, and generally to support the cause of morality and religion in the neighborhoods where they are formed. What constitutes membership is defined by the will of the associates, and what shall be the rights of members is also the subject of their agreement. They are not to be assimilated to parishes, for they have ordinarily no geographical limits. Being voluntary associations they may adopt such rules for their government as their wishes may dictate, subject only to such restrictions as their charters may impose upon them, if they are incorporated. Many religious societies in this country are incorporated. Many others have no corporate existence. In most of the States statutes have been enacted providing an easy mode by which religious societies may become incorporated, at small expense, and when no such mode has been adopted the legislature is competent to incorporate them, though it cannot compel their acceptance of a corporate existence. The act of incorporation brings with it very considerable advantages. It endows the corporators with a name, by which they may sue and be sued in the civil courts. It gives them perpetual existence. It enables them, however numerous, to act as one person, and it simplifies greatly their tenure of property. The powers of such corporations are generally defined by their charter, and the officers, or agencies by which they are permitted to act are also defined. They are almost always allowed to hold property for the use of the society and the church connected with it, and generally to manage the church temporalities. But an incorporated religious society is not an *ecclesiastical* corporation, in the sense of the English law. Such an organization is composed of spiritual persons, and its object is also spiritual. A religious society incorporated is regarded, with us, as a civil corporation, as much so as is a railroad company, a bank, or an insurance company. Hence it is governed by the law precisely as other corporations are. It is subject to visitation, as others are. Intrusion into its offices may be remedied by an appeal to the civil courts, and it will be restrained from appropriation of the property held by it to other uses than those to subserve which it was created. It would be impossible, in the time which I have, to state minutely the provisions of law respecting such corporations. They differ greatly in the different States, because the provisions of the charters are various, and because they have been more or less the subjects of State legislation. I can do no more than call attention to some things in regard to which there is general concurrence of opinion. A religious corporation may take, either by deed or will, real and personal property to an amount limited by law. The statutes of the States, inheriting the jealousy of large accumulation of property in the hands of ecclesiastical persons and religious houses which was so great an evil in England before, and even subsequent to the Reformation, have in many cases enacted that no religious society shall be incorporated, with power to hold property yielding a greater annual income than a specified sum. Of course, where this is the law of the State, property acquired by such a corporation beyond the sum limited is liable to escheat to the commonwealth. Within that limit there is the same freedom of acquisition which belongs to a natural person. And where property has been held for the use of an unincorporated religious society, it will, upon its subsequent incorporation become vested at once, by force of the law, in that corporate body. No conveyance is necessary. So an agreement with individual members of a society to convey land to them for the site of a church may be enforced after they are incorporated, and a conveyance will be decreed to the corporate body.

Religious corporations are also very frequently authorized to purchase and hold land for a burial-ground or cemetery, and to improve it, though they have generally no power to hold lands for any other than religious uses.

In these rights, as in all others, they are protected by the law, while they are restrained from transgressing the powers vested in them, and especially from perverting the trusts they hold.

A very large portion of the religious societies in the country are unincorporated, and in a few of the States charters cannot be obtained for them. They are therefore not legal entities, recognized as having a legal existence. They can neither sue, nor be sued in civil courts. They cannot hold property directly. Yet they may control property held by others for their use. Donations and grants may be legally made to trustees for the use and benefit of an unincorporated religious society, or for the support of the Gospel ministry in connection with any particular church. Any person capable of disposing of his property can create a trust for such a purpose, and, if the trust is properly created, it will not fail for want of a trustee, for it is a rule in courts of equity that no legal trust shall fail because there is no trustee. In such a case the court will raise up one. This is an important principle often called into requisition where churches and religious societies exist without the aid of corporate charters. In all the States the institutions of religion are regarded as essential to the public well-being, and hence trusts for pious and religious purposes are looked upon with great favor by the courts.

The law of charities, at a very early period in English judicial history, was ingrafted upon the common law, and was held to be applicable to trusts for religious uses; and we have upon this subject adopted generally the maxims of the English law. It is only necessary that a gift, devise, or grant be made to trustees capable of taking the legal estate, and that the objects of the trust be defined, or capable of being ascertained. Even if the trustees be incapable of taking, if the conveyances be for charitable or religious uses, they will be supported by courts of equity. It follows from this that a bequest for the benefit of a religious society, though it names no trustee, is valid. So is a bequest for the benefit of poor ministers of a specified religious denomination, though no persons are appointed to take and distribute the fund. A court of equity will raise up agents to make the distribution. I have not time, however, now to go further into the law of charities as affecting religious societies. The subject is a fruitful and interesting one, but I must reserve what I have to say on this subject for a future occasion. It will be seen that, even when not incorporated, the common law doctrine of trusts for religious purposes affords such associations much protection, and enables them without great embarrassments to support church ordinances.

It is very important, however, in all grants for the use of an unincorporated religious society that the extent of the powers of the trustee should be well defined, and the nature and objects of the trust should be clearly specified. It prevents disagreement and litigation. But if they are not, if they are left indefinite, the trustee may always apply to civil courts of equity for direction, and it will readily and authoritatively be given.

I need hardly add that the law will prevent a perversion of a trust in favor of a religious society, as efficiently as it will protect any other trust, and courts will go very far to ascertain what the trust is. In one case, where a deed had been made for the use of a congregation of Christians, designating the congregation by the name of a sect, or denomination, without any other specification of the religious worship intended, it was held that the intent of the donors, or founders, in that respect, might be implied from their own religious tenets, from the prior and contemporary usage, tenets, and doctrines of the congregation, and from the usage, tenets, and doctrines of the sect, or denomination, to which such congregation belonged. It was also held that in ascertaining the early and contemporary usage and doctrines of such sect, resort might be had to history, and to standard works of theology of an era prior to the origin of the dispute or controversy. This ruling, I apprehend, is in accordance with the general practice of civil courts.

I may not now pursue this subject farther. There are other matters relating to the discipline and property of the church in this country, of which the civil law takes cognizance. The most important are the application of the law of charities, the legal effect of by-laws of religious corporations, the tenure of church property, the rights of pew-holders in church edifices, and other things of a kindred nature. What I have to say respecting these must be reserved for another lecture.

SECOND LECTURE.

Gentlemen of the Seminary :—

ON a former occasion I called your attention to the fact that what civil law lawyers denominate the law of charities has an intimate relation to church property in this country. I propose now to add some remarks respecting the history of this law, and its application by civil courts to the property of churches and religious societies. Its importance can hardly be over-estimated. The law of trusts and the law of charities, closely connected as they are, constitute the protection of our churches, so far as they hold and enjoy property.

It is generally believed, and probably the belief is well founded, that the origin of the law of charities must be sought for in an age long anterior to the time when the common law of England came into existence. It is undoubtedly one of the legacies bequeathed to modern times by Roman civilization. Traces of it are found very early in the decisions of the British courts, though it was not until the reign of Elizabeth that the system of law, now so well understood and so important to the welfare of the community, had grown into any considerable degree of completeness. Charities were known, doubtless, before the Christian era; but, so far as is known, they were not, before that period, the subjects of municipal or civil regulation. In the beginning of the fourth century (A. D. 315), Constantine, the first Christian Roman Emperor, granted permission to his subjects to bequeath their property to the church, and, as a consequence of this permission, such bequests began at once to be very largely made. Indeed almost immediately so much property came by devise into the ownership of the church, for various purposes designated by the donors, or testators, for the erection of buildings, and maintenance of religious houses and orders, as well as for church ornaments and religious uses, that it was felt to be a great social evil, and in the year 364 A D. the Emperor Valentinian felt constrained to enact what is called a mortmain law, the object of which was to prevent the accumulation of lands by religious houses, or religious corporations. The mass of property then consisted in land. For a time Valentinian's law restrained gifts, grants, and devises of lands for religious, pious, or charitable uses. But the restraint was temporary. It gradually relaxed, until in the time of Justinian (A. D. 529), it became a recognized maxim of Roman jurisprudence that legacies to pious uses (which included all legacies destined for works of piety, or charity, whether they related to spiritual or to temporal concerns), were entitled to peculiar favor in the courts, and were to be deemed privileged testaments. In the Roman courts the construction of wills which made charitable dispositions of property, was far more liberal than that given to other wills. Charitable legacies and devises were never permitted to be lost in consequence of either the uncertainty, or failure, of the objects for which the testators destined them. Thus, if a legacy or devise was given to the church generally, or to the poor generally, without any specification of the particular church, or without designation of what poor were intended, the law and the courts sustained the gift by awarding the property to the church of the parish or neighborhood in which the testator lived, or to the hospital of the place. In the time of Justinian it was a common usage to give by will a legacy to God, and in such cases the courts construed the legacy to enure to the parish. Whenever the objects of the testator's bounty were indefinite, the legacy, if intended for a charitable use, was carried into effect by the court, and the judge designated the persons to whom the bounty should be applied. More extraordinary still, if a legacy or devise was given for a definite charitable object, which had been previously accomplished, or which had failed, it was nevertheless held valid, and the property given was, at the discretion of the court, applied to some other object, supposed to be cognate. For illustration, if a testator had left a legacy for building a parish church, or for a new apartment in a hospital, and before his death, the church, or the new apartment had been built, or, in the opinion of the judge, was not necessary, or useful, the legacy was not allowed to fail, but it was applied to some other object of piety, or of charity, designated by the judge, and, perhaps, never thought of by the testator.

These principles of the Roman law were, at a very early age, quite as soon as wills were permitted, introduced into the common law of England, though, perhaps, shorn of some of their extravagances.

The early English chancellors were priests and bishops of the Roman Catholic Church. It was not until the reign of Edward Third, (A. D. 1340), that the first lay chancellor was appointed. It was very natural, it ought to have been expected, that when those who had the charge of the estates and testaments of all decedents—those who admitted all wills to probate, and who had control over all executors and administrators, were ecclesiastics—it was natural that a system so favorable to the church as the Roman law of charities should meet with approval, and should be adopted as the law of the realm. It was so adopted. I do not say that all the perversions of testamentary intent, which were tolerated by the Roman law, were ever repeated in the judicial history of England, but many of them were, and, certainly prior to the reign of Queen Elizabeth, the construction given by the chancellors to charitable bequests was sometimes alarmingly unreasonable—practically indeed, a substitution of the will of the judge for the will of the testator. Since that reign there has been less extravagance, but there is still a disposition to go great lengths in sustaining and directing the application of testamentary dispositions which, in the judgment of the law, are regarded as charities. The action of courts of equity in regard to such dispositions has always been exceptional. Grants, bequests, or devises for religious or charitable uses are upheld, when similar grants, bequests, and devises, for other uses not charitable, would fail.

To show how great the favor extended to charitable gifts is, I mention some decisions recorded in the books. They are to the following effect. Generally, if a testator give his property to such person as he shall hereafter name as his executor, and afterward he appoints no executor, or if he appoint one and the person appointed die in the life-time of the testator, the gift will fail. Courts hold that in such a case there is no person to take. But if a like bequest be given to an executor in favor of, or in trust for, a charitable use, the gift will be sustained, though no executor be named. Equity will supply an executor to effectuate the charitable intent of the donor. So if a bequest be given to persons to distribute in charity, and they all die before the will takes effect, the bequest will be enforced, though it would have failed if made to the same persons for their own use. It is upon this principle that devises to persons incapable of taking are upheld, when made for religious or charitable purposes. And, generally, it may be said to be well established that if a devise or a bequest be for a charity, it matters not how uncertain the objects or persons to be benefited may be, if any mode is appointed by which they can be designated; nor whether they are *in esse*, or not, or whether the legatee or devisee be a corporation capable of taking, or not. Civil courts will sustain the gift and carry it into effect. Such is now the law in England, and equally the law in this country.

I have already called attention to the fact that church property is regarded by the law as property devoted to charitable uses. Observe now some of the operations of the law of charities upon church rights of property, as that law is administered by civil courts. It will be seen that its importance can hardly be over-estimated. A devise of property to an unincorporated religious society, or even to a deceased person for the use of such a society, is good, and it will be established in a court of equity. It has been decided that a gift to the "Monthly Meeting of Friends, of Philadelphia," to be held by the meeting as a fund for the distribution of good books among poor people in the back parts of Pennsylvania, was a valid bequest. This is a significant illustration of the great value which the law of charities has in its application to religious societies. The monthly meeting was not incorporated. It was a mere voluntary religious association. It was incapable of taking or holding property for ordinary uses, but it was regarded as competent to take, as the trustee of a charity. And what could have been more indefinite than the description of the beneficiaries? They were poor people in the back parts of Pennsylvania. Many other similar decisions have been made, and I understand it to be the established law throughout the country that unincorporated religious societies may hold and manage property devised to them for religious uses, and may even hold as trustees for charities of which they are made the almoners. True, they cannot be legal trustees, but courts of equity will protect them in the enjoyment of such rights, and, when necessary, will raise up legal trustees, through whom they may act.

And it is not necessary, as I have already intimated, that the beneficiaries of the charity be certainly defined, provided there be a discretionary power vested somewhere over the application of the property, and a religious society, though unincorporated, may be the appointed agent to direct, at its discretion, such application.

So it has been ruled in courts of law that a charitable bequest directly to beneficiaries, enures in some cases to the church organization that has those beneficiaries in charge. Thus a gift to the poor of a church, or religious society, is construed to be a gift to the church or society itself, in trust, to distribute among its poor, and the church is entitled to claim the fund. A gift to the mission and schools of the Episcopal Church, about to be established at Port Cresson (Africa), was held to be a gift in ease of The Domestic and Foreign Missionary Society of the Protestant Episcopal Church which established those schools, and the legacy was decreed to that society. The law regards the substance rather than the words of the gift, and in favor of a charity vests it in the party capable of taking it—in the party in whose ease it was given.

So when there is a defect in the deed, or will, by which a charitable use has been attempted to be created, either in naming the party intended to be the trustee, or in describing the beneficiaries for whom the use was designed, courts of equity will supply the defect, when it can be supplied, "ut res magis valeat, quam pereat." Cases often occur in which a testator has misnamed the church, or religious society, for which he intended the legacy, but if the court can ascertain with reasonable certainty what society he had in view, the legacy will be sustained, and adjudged to the corporation or society manifestly intended. *Thus*, a bequest made to the "trustees, or those who hold the funds of the Theological Seminary at Princeton, New Jersey," was decided to be a gift to the "trustees of the Theological Seminary of the Presbyterian Church at Princeton," the latter being the corporate name. This was because there was no other body answering to the description, and the corporation was generally known as The Theological Seminary at Princeton. Legacies for charitable uses, however, sometimes fail for want of a proper description of the legatee, and therefore extreme caution should always be exercised in gifts or grants to religious societies, as well as in conveyances to any benevolent organization, that the donee, or grantee, be correctly described. If the intended donee, or grantee, is a corporation, it has a name given to it by its charter, a name by which it is known in the law, and that name should always be used. It is unsafe to employ only a part of it.

But, indulgent as the law of charities is, it is proper I should remark that legacies to religious societies will not be sustained, if they require the property, or any part of it, to be held for perpetual accumulation. Churches, I know, are not prone to hold property for unending accumulation, or for accumulation at all, but gifts are some-made for such a purpose. Perpetuities of accumulation, however, are the abhorrence of the law, and they are not tolerated even to support a charity.

I may also notice some statutes that

exist in England, and some that are in force in many of the States of our own federal union. The British statutes of mortmain are not generally in force in this country, but their spirit pervades our common law, and there are enactments of many of our legislatures, intended to protect the sick and infirm against improvident charitable dispositions of their property, near the close of life. These enactments declare in substance that no charitable devise or bequest shall have effect as a testamentary disposition unless made more than a prescribed time before the testator's death. In some of the States this period is fixed at thirty days; in others it is extended to one year. These are the only restraints that occur to me now upon the right to settle property for the use of religious and charitable associations, except that when such associations are incorporated, they are, as I have already remarked, sometimes prohibited by the law of their being from holding property, greater in amount, or of a larger annual value than the sum mentioned in their charters, or prescribed by the statute law of the State.

Before leaving this subject I will add a few observations that may appear somewhat irrelevant to it. What I have said is enough to show that the peculiar law of charities is very closely related to church property, especially to its acquisition and use. But the question may occur to you, What is a charity, in contemplation of law? We know what it is in common understanding, but what is its legal meaning? I shall not attempt to answer the inquiry fully. It would require more time than I can now devote to it. A charity has a much wider significance in civil law than it has in the popular conception. It is enough for my present purpose to say that in this country gifts or settlements for religious uses have always been considered charities. And no matter how the property is acquired, if the purpose of its acquisition be the erection of a church, or the maintenance or propagation of religion, the law regards it as settled for a charitable use. Such was not always the law in England. Even after the Reformation, some such gifts were denied to be charities, and in the spirit of religious intolerance that prevailed, they were declared to be "gifts for superstitious uses." As such they were condemned by the courts, and adjudged to be void. Indeed, one object of the remarkable statute of the 43d Elizabeth, undoubtedly was to distinguish between charitable uses, recognized by law, and superstitious uses. The uses declared by the courts to be superstitious, were generally those created by Roman Catholics, or by Jews. Thus a legacy to certain priests and chapels, that the testatrix might have the benefit of their prayers and masses,—a bequest for educating and bringing up poor children in the Roman Catholic faith,—a bequest by a Jew to "apply and dedicate the revenues thereof toward establishing a Jesuba, or assembly for reading the law, and instructing people in our holy religion," were all held to be for superstitious uses. Such decisions, however, were not directed against Romanists and Jews only. Non-conformists were were also under the ban. In one case, a clergyman of the established church bequeathed to Mr. Baxter $600, to be distributed by him to sixty poor ejected ministers, saying he did not give it them for the sake of their non-conformity, but because he knew many of them to be pious and good men, and in great want. He also gave £20 more to Mr. Baxter, to be laid out in a book, called Baxter's Call to the Unconverted. Strangely enough, Lord Keeper North decided these legacies to be for superstitious uses, and therefore void. It is true this decision was afterward set aside, and it is probable that all these legacies would now be regarded as charities, even in England. Certainly they would in this country.

But it is far from being clear that with us a gift for an irreligious, or even an infidel use, could be sustained. In the well known case of Vidal *vs.* Girard's executors, decided in 1844, by the Supreme Court of the United States, the court sustained as a charity, a devise for the establishment of a college for orphans wherein the testator directed and enjoined that no ecclesiastic, missionary, or minister of any sect whatsoever, should ever hold or exercise any station or duty, and that no such person should ever be admitted for any purpose, or as a visitor within the premises appropriated to the purposes of the said college. The devise was vigorously attacked by most eminent counsel, on the ground that the plan of education directed by it was derogatory to the Christian religion, tending to weaken men's respect for it, and their conviction of its importance, subverting the only foundation of public morals, and therefore mischievous and undesirable. On the other side the devise was defended by equally eminent counsel; and it was denied that such was the tendency of the plan. But throughout the whole argument, as well as in the opinion of the court, it appears to have been assumed that had the will been truly obnoxious to the objection urged against it, had it intended the establishment of an irreligious or infidel college, the devise might not have been a valid charity. That indeed was not the decision, but the case leans in that direction. And in two cases at least in the highest courts of two of the States, it has been more than intimated that a gift in trust for the support and propagation of irreligion and infidelity cannot be supported. I do not perceive how it could be, as a charity, entitled to the protection of the law of charities.

But I have dwelt too long upon this

subject. My apology must be that in the law of charities is found the chief protector of church property, and, when associated with the law of trusts, the chief regulator.

I invite your attention now to some matters which relate to the tenure by which church property may be held. Upon this subject not much is needed. The simplest, and, as I have heretofore said, the best mode of holding such property is by the agency of a corporation whenever the laws of the States permit the incorporation of religious societies. The powers of such a corporation are, of course, only those which are conferred by its charter, it being a well settled principle of law that no corporation is deemed to possess any other power than that which is expressly granted, or given by necessary implication. In obtaining a charter, therefore, while it is undesirable that much detail of regulation should be inserted in it, it is important that it should confer all necessary powers to hold and manage property for the uses intended. Corporate organization not only gives perpetual legal existence to an artificial being, capable of taking, holding, and managing both real and personal property, but it enables all the corporators to act as an unit in all matters in which they are interested relating to the purposes of their organization. To a church, or religious society, incorporated, lands or other property may be directly conveyed, and when thus conveyed, they may be used freely and unrestrictedly, except that they cannot be diverted to other objects than those for which the property was at first destined. But I think it may be laid down as true, that an incorporated religious society would not be permitted by the law to hold property for any other than religious or charitable uses. Such a holding would be regarded as foreign to the purposes for which the corporate existence was given. While a grant, or a devise, might be made to it for the support of the Gospel, or for any religious use, or, *perhaps*, for any use that the law recognizes as charitable, it could not be made a trustee for any use not religious or charitable. Many trusts, known and recognized by the law, are trusts for natural persons and secular purposes. John Stiles holds land in trust for Richard Roe, the latter being entitled to the rents, issues, and profits. Such a trust an incorporated religious society cannot generally hold. Nor can it be the executor of a will, though it may be a devisee, or a legatee.

The charters of church corporations exhibit great varieties. In some, the members of the church itself, and only they, are the corporators. They alone have the right to elect the officers and managers. In others the members of the corporation may be the associates in the religious society, and not necessarily members of the church, for the use of which the corporation is authorized to hold property. In others still, the officers, managers, or agents may be elected or appointed by an external organization, none of the members of which are members of the corporation. In the case of single churches this is not common, but there are such instances in the church at large. The trustees and managers of the corporation, "The trustees of the General Assembly of the Presbyterian Church" are elected, not by any members of the corporation, but by the General Assembly. Some of the boards of the church have no membership. Their officers are appointed by an exterior authority. These differences of structure arise out of the organic laws or charters which have been obtained from the State. They are immaterial to the tenure of the property. They relate rather to its management. It is the corporation that holds the property. In that the title is vested. That only can sue for injuries to it. That only can sell it. Individual members of the church, or even of the corporation, have no legal interest in the property. They may control its use through the corporation, but they are not owners.

A second mode in which church property is often held, is by unincorporated trustees who hold the title for the use of the church, or for the use of a religious society, out of which the church is gathered. Lands, or personal property, may be conveyed by deed or will to a person and his heirs in trust for a specified church or society. The grantee, devisee, or donee, in such a case is the owner in law, though he has no beneficial interest. The whole beneficial use is in the church or society as fully as if they were the absolute owners. Yet he alone can sue in a court of law for trespasses upon the property, and he alone can make title to others in case of a sale. If he dies, the ownership descends to his heir-at-law, clothed however with the same trusts with which his ancestor held it. If there be two or more trustees, the ownership, on the death of one passes to the survivor or survivors, and on the death of the last survivor descends to his heir-at-law, who will be compelled to allow such use of the property as the religious society may direct, not inconsistent with the purposes for which the grant was first made.

A third mode in which church property is sometimes held is by the agency of two co-operating corporations, one, the religious society with power to elect and employ a minister, collect dues, and hold property directly as the property of the society, and the other, having also power to acquire, manage, and dispose of lands, and personality in trust for the benefit of the society. This is a cumbrous system, but it is sometimes selected for the supposed reason that as each of these dual corporations performs a somewhat different office, they act as checks upon each other, and that thus property may be held and perpetually devoted to religious uses, with less danger of its being squandered by those for whose use it is held, and with less risk of its being seized, or sold on execution for liabilities incurred. In my opinion such a complex arrangement adds little, if anything to the security of the property, and it must be attended with many embarrassments.

A fourth mode in which church property is held, is by an unincorporated religious association without known trustees. A person may undoubtedly give by will both personalty and realty to an unincorporated religious society, without the intervention of named trustees, and the law will sanction the gift. Whether lands can be granted directly to such a society by deed, may admit of considerable doubt. Legal form is not so essential in a will as it is in a deed. The law recognizes the fact that a testator when making his will may be infirm, and "inops consilii," destitute of legal counsel. A will therefore sometimes has an operation which a deed using the same words would not have. But, though an unincorporated religious society may hold property devised or bequeathed to it for pious purposes, and, *possibly*, property conveyed to it by deed, such a tenure is attended with serious embarrassments. Ordinarily such a society cannot sell its property. It cannot make a deed. Of course it can make no disposition of it by will. It is always embarrassed in protecting its own enjoyment. It cannot sue for trespasses upon the property. Courts of equity, it is true, will raise up trustees for the protection of such societies, and in some of the States statutes have given to them a quasi corporate existence. But prudence and convenience alike dictate that in all cases where an unincorporated religious society desires to acquire and to hold property of any nature, the legal ownership thereof should be vested in trustees for the use of the society. Such trustees have power to protect the property, to sue for injuries to it, and, under the direction of the society, to sell and convey it. At the same time they are amenable to courts of law. They may be compelled to account, and they may be restrained from any violation of their trust.

There is still another mode in which property is largely held in this country for religious, or church uses. In the Moravian congregations the property devoted to pious uses is held neither by a corporation nor by trustees, nor yet by the congregation itself. In some of the congregations, and I presume in all, the title to the churches, school-houses, and cemeteries is held by the bishop, who transmits it by will to his successor in office. And such is the tenure of most Roman Catholic churches in the country. The title to the real estate resides in the bishop of the diocese. In a certain sense he is a trustee thereof for religious uses, but there is no declaration of trust, and he controls the enjoyment, and transmits the title by devise. The purpose of this arrangement is to exclude the laity from that power of interference which they would have were the title vested in a corporation. But inasmuch as the holders of such titles are not corporations, either sole or aggregate, as are the English bishops, deans, and even parsons, lands, held by them, do not pass to their successors in office, unless through the instrumentality of a deed, or will.

These are the most common modes in which property is holden for religious or church uses. Whatever mode, other than the last mentioned, may be selected, it is of great importance that the instrument (whether it be a deed, or a will), by which the property is acquired, should recognize the distinctive character of the organization for the benefit of which the conveyance is to be made. The reasons for this will appear from what I said in my former lecture. It is necessary in order to prevent a possible perversion of the property from the uses for which its acquisition was intended.

1. If the church organization is a separate and independent one, at liberty to form and change its order, and articles of faith, having no connection with other churches, or associated with others only for counsel, and at liberty to dissolve even that association at its pleasure, a conveyance to it, or for its use generally, is all that is needed. The property is thus put under the control of a majority of the congregation, and its uses may change with the changing creed or order of the church.

2. But if the church be independent, and yet it is designed that the property conveyed to it, or in trust for it, shall be devoted to the maintenance and propagation of certain doctrines, or articles of faith, the deed or will should declare such design explicitly.

3. Or if the purpose be to settle the

property for the use of a church, or religious society while it remains in connection with and subject to the authority of some larger ecclesiastical body, the conveyance should recognize the connection and the subordination intended. A failure to observe these precautions, and to indicate clearly and distinctively in the muniments of title to church property the precise uses which the property is intended to subserve, has often encouraged division and given rise to unhappy litigation. And it cannot be doubted that very many titles are held for church purposes in full confidence that they secure the teaching of some particular doctrines, or systems of faith, or that they are for the benefit of some particular denomination, or a church subject to a known higher ecclesiastical authority, when in fact, they may consistently with law be converted to quite different purposes.

Having thus called your attention to the various modes in which church property may be held I proceed to consider how it may be acquired, or rather, what are the usual evidences of title to it. Upon this subject little need be said, for, generally, the modes of acquisition do not differ from those by which natural persons, and corporations, acquire rights to property. The evidence of right or title is not, however, always found in a deed or a will.

In some cases the law presumes a grant, when none was ever actually made. When there has been an actual and continuous occupation by a religious society, of a lot of ground, for religious uses, without any recognition of right to the lot in any other person, and when that occupancy has been continued during a period equal to the statutory period of limitation in the State (varying in the different States from seven to twenty-one years), courts of law sometimes presume that a grant was made by the former owners to the occupants, and this presumption may be conclusive of the right. Even if not, the statute itself will protect the continued enjoyment. Instances not a few exist, especially in the rural districts of the older States, in which this is the only evidence that a religious society has, of title to the church property it occupies. It is applicable not only to the ground upon which a church edifice may be erected, but also to privileges on adjoining property, to passage-ways to and from the church, and to easements necessary and convenient to the purposes of its enjoyment. Legal presumptions, recognized both in courts of law and of equity, are invaluable for giving security to church titles.

Another mode of acquiring church property is by license from the owner. In some cases the proprietor of land has given permission to a religious society, or church organization, to build a church edifice upon his property. Such a license may be either verbal or written. In either case it may be revoked before the licenses have done anything under it. But when, in reliance upon it, they have proceeded and made expenditures upon the property, in the erection of a building, it is not in the power of the owner to withdraw his permission, and resume the possession of the land. The license executed has become a contract, and a muniment of right. And a license is sometimes presumed from the conduct of the party who had a right to give it. Thus if the true owner of a lot of ground should see a religious society begining to build upon it, under a mistaken belief of its members that they had a right there to build and if, with knowledge of their belief, he should remain silent, the law would not permit him to claim the property after the building was erected. It would be presumed he had licensed, or permitted the erection, and, as he did not speak when he should have spoken, he would not be permitted to speak afterward.

Closely allied to acquisitions by license are acquisitions by dedication. The common law allows the devotion by dedication of property to religious and charitable uses, such as for church lots, cemeteries, and other like purposes. Indeed, an owner of property may give his land for any public use. This he may do either by parol, or in writing, and courts of law will protect the gift. And it is not necessary that the religious society intended to be benefited should be in being when the dedication is made. Whenever afterward it comes into existence, the anterior dedication will enure to its benefit, if the society's objects accord with the purpose of the donor, and it can be gathered that he contemplated a use by such a society.

Of the other and more common modes of acquiring church property, such as by deed, or by will, by absolute or conditional grants or devises for a limited time, I need say nothing, since they are familiar to every one. And there is nothing in the acquisition of personal property for church purposes that requires particular notice.

Before leaving this branch of my subject I may add that the right of a church organization to acquire and hold lands for religious uses, ordinarily carries with it the right to sell the property thus holden, and make title therefor to a purchaser. It does not, however, in all cases. When real estate is held under a license or a dedication for a specific religious use, the religious society holding it cannot lawfully sell it for any other use. Certainly they they cannot without the consent of the donor, unless aided by authority given by the legislature of the State, and I think it may well be doubted whether such a power can be conferred by legislative authority. And in all cases where the power to alienate exists, the conveyance must be made by the person, or persons, the corporation or the trustees in whom the legal title is vested.

I come next to the subject of internal regulation of religious societies by by-laws. When such a society is unincorporated, it generally has articles of association, by which its elections, its meetings, and the conduct of its temporal affairs are regulated. Substantial conformity to the requirements of those articles is essential to the valid transaction of any of its business. The articles may be changed from time to time, by the consent of the associates, but while they exist they are controlling.

When a religious society is incorporated, its charter is its fundamental law, and that confers upon it power, either expressly or by necessary implication, to make by-laws for the regulation of its internal management. By-laws of such corporations generally refer to the times and conduct of meetings of the corporators, to the number and duties of the officers, to the times and mode of conducting the elections, and to the qualifications of the electors, unless these matters are regulated by the charter. There are also many other matters relating to the corporate action, in relation to which by-laws may be made. The power of making by-laws resides only in those in whom it is vested by the charter; but if that instrument is silent upon the subject, the power may be exercised by the members of the corporation at large. It is always a limited power. No by-law is of any force which conflicts with the charter, or with the law of the land. Nor is any by-law valid which does not relate to the legitimate purposes of the corporation. If the charter has prescribed who shall be entitled to vote at any corporate meeting, the right of such persons to vote cannot be restricted or taken away by any by-law. Yet, if the language of the charter is only negative, the rule is different. Let me illustrate. If the charter declares that only members of the church who have been such twelve months preceding the election, shall have a vote in the choice of church officers, it is lawful to adopt a by-law declaring that no member of the church whose pew-rent has been in arrears six months shall be entitled to a vote. Such a by-law and the charter are not in conflict with each other. Very often the charter makes no provision respecting voters. In such cases, the members of the corporation may determine by a by-law who may vote, and for what officers. A by-law that only communing members of the church shall have a voice in the choice of a minister, or other church officers, is good. So is one that allows both male and female members to vote, or confines the elective right to one sex. So is one that contributors or pew-holders alone shall be electors. A by-law that all members of the church, or of the church and society, may vote, does not extend to infants, or persons under the age of twenty-one years. Neither in civil nor in religious corporations are infants allowed by the common law to vote, unless such right is expressly given to them by the charter, though perhaps, if the charter is silent on this subject, the right might be conferred by express words in a by-law. Voting by proxy is not allowable, unless the charter permits it. All by-laws lawfully made in pursuance of the power conferred by the charter are as binding upon every member of the corporation as is the charter itself.

them as it is held in this country. In England, the law of church seats in the cathedrals, the parish churches, and in the chapels of ease, is complicated and often difficult to be understood. Even seat rights in private and proprietary chapels have frequently been the subjects of controversy. In the church edifices erected under the church building acts of parliament (more than twenty in number), seat rights are regulated by statute, and some of the regulations are novel. But to attempt an exhibition of the law governing seat rights in the different classes of English churches would require much time, and it would be alien from my purpose, which is to speak generally of the law in this country. I confess some inclination to refer to the history of the introduction of pews into churches, for to me it is extremely interesting. But I must resist the temptation. Let me refer those of you who have curiosity upon the subject, to "Heale's Law of Church Seats," published in London in 1872, where you will find much that is amusing as well as instructive, though the book relates almost exclusively to pews, or seats, in buildings of the English Established Church. In this country where, as we have seen, the ownership of church property is generally vested either in a corporation, or in trustees who hold for the use of a religious society, or of a church organization, it may be regarded as the common rule that pews belong to the legal owners of the church building. And the right of an individual holder of a pew is not, in any just sense, partial ownership of the building itself. It is not ownership of the ground on which the pew rests. The sale of a pew, as a pew, conveys no such ownership. The pew-holder's right is incorporeal, a mere easement, as the law denominates it, or, at most, an unfructuary interest; in its nature something like the right one man may have to pass over the land of another—a privilege upon the land, but not ownership of it.

The right to a pew being thus limited, it does not interfere with the power of the corporation, or of the trustee, to take down the church and rebuild. The holder of the pew takes his right, subject to such changes as the altered circumstances of the congregation require. His consent is not necessary to such change, and when the church edifice is taken down and a new one is erected in its place, his right is extinguished. He is not entitled to a pew in the new building merely because he was a pew-holder in the old. But while his right remains it is exclusive. He may use the pew on all occasions when the church is open; whether for worship, or for any other purpose. He may, if he will, put a fastening on the door of his pew, and deny access to it to all persons other than those whom he chooses to admit. He may even maintain an action at law against an intruder.

The mode of acquisition of pew rights in this country is very simple. It is either by perpetual grant from the owners of the church edifice, whoever they may be, or it is by demise for a limited term. In some churches the pews are sold, in others they are let from year to year, and in others still they are free. Pews in the parish churches of England are very often held by prescription, that is, in virtue of the fact that the possession has been enjoyed by the holder, or those to whose right he has succeeded (using the quaint language of old judges), "from the time whereof the memory of man runneth not to the contrary." Other pew rights are appurtenant to the ownership of landed estates in the vicinity, and others still belong to the incumbents of certain offices by virtue of their incumbency. I know of no such titles to pews in this country, and certainly they are undesirable.

All pew rights are, of course, subject to such quit-rents, or assessments, as were stipulated for, or were existing when the rights were granted, and an action at law may be maintained against the holder or occupant for the recovery of those rents. These rents cannot, however, be raised during the continuance of the holder's right, without his consent, unless the power to raise them was reserved in the grant. It is not essential to the liability of a pew-holder for the rent that he has actually occupied the pew. His holding the right is sufficient to make him a debtor for the rent.

Of course when the right to a pew has been created by a lease for a defined period, it will terminate at the expiration of that period, but when the pew has been sold to a purchaser, his right, unless surrendered, will continue so long as the church stands and is used for church purposes. On the death of the owner, it devolves upon either his heirs, or legatees, or devisees, or upon his personal representatives. Whether in the event of failure to dispose of it by will it passes to the heirs, or to the executors or administrators, depends upon the question whether by law of the State in which the church edifice is situated, pew rights are real or personal property. This is sometimes determined by statute, but when it is not, there has been a difference of opinion in the courts. In some of the States pews are considered real property, as in Connecticut and Maine. In such cases the pew descends to the heir-at-law. In other States pews are regarded as personal property, and on the death of the owners they vest in his executors or administrators, unless disposed of by his will. Such is the law of Massachusetts and New Hampshire, and I think of most of the States. In New York the decisions of the courts have left the subject in some doubt, and I will not venture to express an opinion respecting it. It is important to the church, or religious society, only as it determines who is responsible for the pew rents accruing after the decease of a pew-holder, though in Pennsylvania it has been decided that when pews descend to executors, they are not liable for pew rents accruing after the death of their testator. I doubt whether such would be held to be the law elsewhere.

Thus far, you will have observed, my remarks have been directed principally to the law as it affects the property of single church organizations. A denomination of Christians, however, consisting of many church organizations, may own property, as a single body. It may own a theological seminary, or buildings for the convenience of its benevolent operations, or a fund for the promotion of its interests. These and other kinds of property may belong to it, as a whole; may be acquired in the same manner, held by the same tenure, and controlled and regulated by the same law of trusts and charities. So there are benevolent and religious associations, happily many in number, which are adjutants of the churches, and which receive and control large amounts of property, though they are not subordinate to any church authority. They, too, are protected in the enjoyment of their property, aided in its acquisition, and controlled in its disposition by the civil law, by the same law of charities and trusts which is the shield and regulator of the humblest church organization.

I have not time to consider fully the law relating to the powers and duties of church officers. I mean the officers of a church as distinguished from the officers of the corporation, or religious society, that holds the property. Nor is such a consideration essential to the object I have in view. The powers and duties of the ministers, the elders, the deacons, the vestrymen, and the bishops, are subjects of definition and regulation rather by ecclesiastical than civil law. There are, however, a few matters, relative to the civil rights and duties of ministers as such, that it may be well to notice. In some of the States, regulations have been prescribed by statutes respecting the solemnization of marriage by clergymen, as well as respecting the registration of such marriages, and the registration of baptisms and burials. What these are I do not propose to say. They differ with the statutes of the several States, and it would require much time to mention them in detail. But there are some particulars not affected by local statutes, to which I may, perhaps not unprofitably, allude. It has occurred that an unhappy conflict has arisen between parental authority and the action of a Christian minister. I may illustrate what I mean by referring to a real case actually decided in one of our courts. The circumstances, briefly stated, were these. A Baptist clergyman of good standing was prohibited by a father from administering the ordinance of Baptism, by immersion, to his minor daughter, aged seventeen, she having been previously baptized in the Presbyterian Church to which her mother belonged. The clergyman, however, disregarding the express prohibition of the father, baptized the daughter a few Sabbaths afterward, by immersing her, and the question was raised whether his act was not a violation of law. The court decided that it was, and inflicted a penalty upon him. The reasons given for the decision were that the act of the clergyman was an interference with the lawful authority of the father over the child during her minority; that the authority of the father results from his duties; that he is charged with the duties of maintenance and education; that these duties cannot be performed without authority to command and enforce obedience; that the duty to educate requires, proper attention to religious culture, and that, in the discharge of this duty, it is the clear right of the father to designate such teachers in morals and religion, as he may think best fitted to give correct instruction. From this it seemed to the court to follow that, though a father cannot force a child to adopt religious opinions contrary to the dictates of the child's conscience, if he should come to the conclusion, the attendance of his child upon the ministrations of any particular religious instructor was not conducive to its welfare, he might prohibit such attendance; and confine it to such religious teachers as he might select, and that any interference with the exercise of this authority amounted to an invasion of his legal rights. This decision met some criticism at the time it was made, but it was accepted by eminent lawyers and judges, as well as by others, as a true exposition of the law. It is understood to have had the approval of Chancellor Kent.

It is equally true that masters have a right to control the religious education of their apprentices, and direct what religious services they shall attend. With this right neither ministers of religion, nor any other persons, can lawfully interfere.

The question has sometimes been agitated whether a clergyman, when called as a witness in a court of law, may refuse to disclose matters which have been confidentially communicated to him by persons under his religious teaching. The general rule in this country is that he cannot. There are some communications which the law regards as privileged, and which the person who has received them is not at liberty to disclose. Such are those made by a client to his legal counsel. But neither penitential confessions made to a minister, nor even secrets confided to a Roman Catholic priest in the confessional, are considered privileged communications, which the minister or priest may not be compelled to reveal. Some modifications of this rule have, it is true, been made by statute. A law of the State of New York enacts that no minister of the Gospel, or priest of any denomination whatsoever, shall be allowed to disclose any confessions made to him in his professional character, in the course of discipline enjoined by the rules or practice of such denomination. But even under this law, the confession is privileged only when it has been received in the course of church discipline. The general rule elsewhere is as I have stated it.

I have no time to say more. In what I have said, my object has been to state generally what I understand to be the rules of civil law, in this country, applicable to church polity, discipline, and property. I have aimed only to gather from the great mass of decisions of Federal and State courts, as well as from the statutes of the States, the conclusions which have been reached, without endeavoring to state the reasons which have led to those conclusions. And I have passed unnoticed many distinctions recognized by the courts, and important to be understood by every lawyer. I am not speaking to lawyers, or to those who intend entering the legal profession. I am addressing those who look forward to the Christian ministry, and endeavouring to communicate that knowledge which they ought to possess—a knowledge of general principles. I am fully aware that all which I have stated as my understanding of these general principles does not meet universal acceptance. There is a want of harmony in the decisions of the courts of the different States. Doctrines are advanced by some which are denied by others. I have sought only to spread before you those doctrines which, in my judgment, are supported by a preponderance of authority, and by the soundest reasoning. And I think there is manifest in the action of the numerous courts of the country a tendency toward greater harmony of decisions upon the subjects we have been considering than formerly existed. The relation of municipal law to church polity, discipline, and property, is becoming better understood; and there is less conflict of judgment than there was.

I detain you no longer. Fully sensible as I am that what has been said is not a full exposition of the subject to which your attention has been called, and that it will not make you lawyers, it has, I hope, revealed to you something that you may hereafter find convenient and useful.

www.ingramcontent.com/pod-product-compliance
Lightning Source LLC
LaVergne TN
LVHW021413110826
845150LV00007B/1898

* 9 7 8 1 4 2 5 5 1 0 8 5 5 *